WHY SHOULD I EAT WELL?

B.E.S.
PUBLISHING

Books in the
WHY SHOULD I? Series:

WHY SHOULD I Protect Nature?   WHY SHOULD I Eat Well?
WHY SHOULD I Recycle?   WHY SHOULD I Help?
WHY SHOULD I Save Water?   WHY SHOULD I Listen?
WHY SHOULD I Save Energy?   WHY SHOULD I Share?

First edition for the United States, its territories and dependencies,
and Canada published in 2005 by B.E.S. Publishing

First published in Great Britain in 2001 by Hodder Wayland, an imprint
of Hodder Children's Books.
© Copyright 2001 Hodder Wayland
Hodder Children's Books
A division of Hodder Headline Ltd.

All inquiries should be addressed to:
B.E.S. Publishing
250 Wireless Boulevard
Hauppauge, NY 11788
www.bes-publishing.com

ISBN-13:978-0-7641-3217-9

Library of Congress Catalog Card Number 2004113859

Printed in China
18 17 16 15 14 13

Date of Manufacture : January 2019
Manufactured by : Shenzhen Wing King Tong Paper Products Co. Ltd.,
Shenzhen, Guangdong, China

WHY SHOULD I EAT WELL?

Written by Claire Llewellyn

Illustrated by Mike Gordon

B.E.S.
PUBLISHING

Rachel and I love eating well.

fresh
milk

chicken

We make every meal a feast.

sweet grapes

tasty lettuce

juicy tomatoes

crunchy apples

crisp radishes

crusty bread

Before I met Rachel, I didn't eat like I do now.

fatty burgers

fatty french fries

fatty potato chips

hot, cheesy pizza

I always ate the same kinds of food.

sweet cupcakes

soda

sweet cookies

sweet, fatty doughnuts

candy

sweet cake

Everyone eats food like this sometimes.

It tastes sweet ...

and it is always easy to find.

People tried to interest me in other kinds of food. They tried to make me eat well.

My Dad tried ...

The lunch lady tried ...

11

And so did Grandpa and my Mom ...

13

But then a new girl came to
our school ...

At lunchtime, she chose the salad.

Rachel told me that eating well
means eating lots of different foods.

She said, "Guess what will happen if you have lots of sugary drinks?"

"You'll get pimples and your teeth will decay."

Then she said, "And what do you think will happen if you never eat fresh fruit or vegetables?"

"You'll catch every cough and cold."

And she said, "What if you eat fatty foods all your life – what do you think will happen to you then?"

"You'll gain weight ...

you won't be fit ...

and – who knows? –
you might even get sick."

So now I eat as
well as Rachel.
Good food gives us
everything we need
to grow and
be healthy.

Good food helps us
to have energy
and zing ...

and to have
clear skin and
shiny hair.

It means that my meals
are more exciting now ...

And I can still have a treat
now and then.

Notes for parents and teachers

Why Should I?

These books will help young readers to recognize what they like and dislike, what is fair and unfair, and what is right and wrong; to think about themselves, learn from their experiences, and recognize what they are good at. Some titles in this series will help to teach children how to make simple choices that improve their health and well-being, to maintain personal hygiene, and to learn rules for, and ways of, keeping safe, including basic road safety. Reading these books will help children recognize how their behavior affects other people, to listen to other people, and play and work cooperatively, and that family and friends should care for one another.

About *Why Should I Eat Well?*

Why Should I Eat Well? is intended to be an enjoyable book that discusses the importance of a healthy diet. From an early age, children make choices about the food they eat. If they know about the value of different foods, they can begin to make real choices to improve their health and well-being. Eating well is one of the ways we look after ourselves. It is important for our self-esteem.

Suggestions as you read the book with children

As you read this book with children, stop now and again to discuss the issues raised in the text. Has anyone ever tried to make them eat something they didn't want or tried to stop them from eating something they did? Why was this? Do they eat school lunches or bring a bag lunch? What kinds of foods do they choose?

Ask children to name their favorite and least favorite foods. This will show how personal their food likes and dislikes can be. Also, our tastes change as we grow older. Are there any foods that they used to dislike that they enjoy eating now?

Try not to dwell exclusively on "healthy" foods. The message of the book is to celebrate food and enjoy its wonderful variety. Eating widely is the secret of a well-balanced diet.

Suggested follow-up activities

Ask the cafeteria for a copy of a weekly menu. Photocopy it for the children, and ask them to think what foods Monica would have chosen before she met Rachel. What would she have chosen afterward?

Have a "New Tastes Day" at school. Ask the children to bring in foods that they have never tasted. They could be radishes, dried apricots, or small pieces of cheese. Display the foods and ask everyone to try something. Can the children describe the taste and texture? Do they like it?

Ask the children to draw a food diary for one day, and then swap it with a friend. Do they think the other person has eaten a good mixture of different types of food. How does their diet compare to the chart on page 16?

Do a project on some kind of food, such as pizza. What ingredients does it contain? How is it made? What are the children's favorite toppings? Ask them to draw a pizza. Visit a local pizzeria to see the different stages in making a pizza.

Play an ABC food game in which they take turns memorizing a list of foods and then add a new one.
"I went to the restaurant, and I ate an apple."
"I went to the restaurant, and I ate an apple and some bread."
"I went to the restaurant, and I ate an apple, some bread, and a piece of cheese."
And so on.

Suggested activities

Why Should I Eat Well? also gives children an opportunity to discuss things they have learned elsewhere.

This book could form the basis for discussions about where food comes from. For example, you could ask children to try to find out where a particular food comes from by reading what it says on the package.

Children could also ask their grandparents or another older person what they used to eat when they were young. Do they think that people were more or less healthy in those days?

Another activity would be to show children the nutrition breakdown on the packages of a few different foods, and see if they can put them in order of healthiness and give reasons for their chosen order.

Books to read

Eating Apples by Gail Saunders-Smith
(Capstone Press, 1998)

Eating Well by Lisa Trumbauer
(Yellow Umbrella Books, 2003)